CHANGING

D0314687

ALSO BY ANNA WOODFORD

POETRY
Birdhouse (Salt 2010)

ANNA WOODFORD

Changing Room

SALT

CROMER

PUBLISHED BY SALT PUBLISHING 2018

2 4 6 8 10 9 7 5 3 1

Copyright © Anna Woodford 2018

Anna Woodford has asserted her right under the Copyright, Designs and Patents Act 1988 to be identified as the author of this work.

This book is sold subject to the condition that it shall not, by way of trade or otherwise, be lent, resold, hired out, or otherwise circulated without the publisher's prior consent in any form of binding or cover other than that in which it is published and without a similar condition including this condition being imposed on the subsequent publisher.

First published in Great Britain in 2018 by
Salt Publishing Ltd
12 Norwich Road, Cromer, Norfolk NR27 0AX United Kingdom

www.saltpublishing.com

Salt Publishing Limited Reg. No. 5293401

A CIP catalogue record for this book is available from the British Library

ISBN 978 1 78463 088 1 (Paperback edition)

Typeset in Sabon by Salt Publishing

Printed and bound in Great Britain by Clays Ltd, Elcograf S.p.A.

Salt Publishing Limited is committed to responsible forest management. This book is made from Forest Stewardship Council™ certified paper.

For Mum and Dad

Contents

Poem for the Archive

Sometimes when I write poetry I wonder
if what I am really doing is writing
my own name over and over
like a kid with a sparkler
or like a kid slumped over
a much scribbled on jotter
today in this library with its vast reserves
and more material still
to be sorted and a new tranche of stuff
due in the spring. The archivist tells me
I am only allowed a pencil;
and what am I doing here but trying
to add something to Poetry? My name?
Behind every line I write I see
how transparent it is Anna Woodford
Anna Woodford Anna Woodford and yet
I can't bring myself to sign off
any other way.

CHANGING ROOM

Changing Room

My hands, like the many hands
of a rabble, are ready with sticks
and stones for my body but today
I appear from all angles in the gilt-
mirrored triptych as something holy.
My new figure is that of a mother.
I would give myself this little room
with its curtain for a closed door.
My own mother whispers to be let in:
an empty stool in a far-off corner
of the cubicle is where I once sat
at her stockinged feet, waiting
and waiting to be a woman.

Mother and Mother and Child

My mother steps out between the parked cars
into the day's hidden traffic: 'I'll be the one
to be hit,' she declares, ready to clear a path
for the baby and me. I nearly let go of the buggy
to hang on to her skirts but wait, long
beyond the locked school gates. The little shield
of my mother's handbag is by her side in the fray.

My mother calls a week later, after only an hour
of babysitting. When I get there it is her I want
to soothe, as much as the baby she hands me
like a baton. I hold my son in my living room
and try to keep my mother, talking
about Saturday or the one after definitely:
pencilling in nights out that are yet to come.

Second Sight

Lying in the unforgiving morning on a low bed
(a year later – packing up –
I found I had been lying on nothing
beyond the rented mattress
but books and old newspapers)
as he lets himself out the inner door
of my flat, then down the flight of stairs
with their threadbare carpet. Listening
in my pit for the final
click which has been coming
since the beginning of our spiralling
arguing. Still my mobile will call
me to call him – to take his leaving back.

A week or so later, I do not know
my life is holding
you in a corner of the bar
where I am being out the house.
Had I seen you cradling our baby
among the pints and dated clouds
of smoke, I might have done
something to upset the delicate
balance of our meeting which
as it happened, happened
right although all the way home I missed
the night's enormity – crying (laughably
now) on my brother's lurching shoulder.

What Archie Gets

An old pram with a fresh sheet
on his three days (the other days
are Daisy B's). A ceiling

hung with cardboard stars.
A rubber egg right
for little hands. Heuristic

play. Toys kept separately
until his immunity builds up.
A third of Hayley. A mother hiding

in the nursery office, practising
being miles away. Next week I will
properly leave my son: he will leap

out at first in the rush
hour, squatted on another woman's
lap or running before

he can walk to school.
At the end of today's
trial he is immersed

in a pool of plastic balls,
grappling with one colourful sphere
like a whole world without me.

Journey

Crossing a road on my own, three days after you
were born, when the beep of the green man turned
into a hundred taxi drivers leaning on their horns.
There were trams, transporters, nuns on horseback,
chattering crocodiles, bandwagons, tuc-tucs, spilled loads –
the road got crosser as I crossed it – wider – until I knew
I could reach the other side before I reached the other side,
leaving you for ten minutes I could leave you forever.

Now we had crawled away from the maw of the hospital
entrance in our family car, how careful I must be!
Your seat in the traffic with its little straps illustrating
like the safety card in an aeroplane seat pocket
in the event of an emergency, how fucked we are.
Wrapped in your receiving blanket, you were enormous
as a body in a rolled-up carpet. I kept looking
over my shoulder to check you were still breathing.

Going round the block the first time you got covered
in money. Tired cafés opened up for us and nearby
shops a street away where there were no streets before.
Town was out of reach as scissors; gated like the stairs
in my safe house which overnight had become
an evangelical church in an ordinary-looking terrace
devoted to the cult of you. Your pram was festooned
as a Spanish *paso*. It was a bash I could just crawl into.

Three years on, your walking makes the journey vast.
I wander beside you with the buggy that was guaranteed
for sand-dunes; snowstorms; all terrain but veers now
to the refurbished playground of my childhood – that strange
no place where you clamber while I clap and watch you
pick up things I half remember. I was thirty-five and late
when I found out you were coming. I ran out the door anyway,
just catching the packed bus before it moved away.

School Run

Like a shopping trolley up to here
with Asda wipes and wonky veg
and blue milk and Cheesestrings
and all of the stuff most like the stuff
I cannot find and eggs on top
trundling along the school run
with my stuck wheel squealing out
its song *Get Up Stop Are We Safe*
To Go and *Look At Me* I am saying
Look At Me Mumming Look At Me
Doing the MumMum with one hand
tied behind my back while still
holding down my coat and job

Teach me Archie Teach me Ethan
Teach me Charlottes S and G
Teach me you who are all bike
who one day will fly but for now
are wobbly in the enormity
of your lit up trainers Teach me
before Topic before assembly
before Miss Smith rounds up
her Clever Crocodiles before Music
before the big machines swallow us
when the sky is thick with God-specks
Teach me the infinite rules of bike train
of fidget spinners O to pick up my kazoo

The Man

He was coming for me across the Niger, the hazy
Zambezi, the Sudetenland that still existed
in my broken-backed school atlas.
He was getting warmer in France.
Under his feet countries were the little people
and bushes scattered around a model railway.
The Man had nearly reached the Todmorden café
where I was sipping from a tumbler, listening to him
over my mother. He was rattling the door
of the bright afternoon when I set
him back in my head. Then The Man started again.

Sometimes my bed was *Knight Rider,* transporting me
like the car lights flashing across the ceiling.
Sometimes The Man was there –
in the bucket that sat by my plastic-sheeted mattress
for years – or leaping out of the seventies wallpaper
whose pattern could never be untangled.
Maybe he was The Man who was always coming
for my grandfather, and who stopped him
going back to Poland. The Man who hunted my family
to the edge of my childhood was still
in the background, just unable to get me.

Swimming Lesson

I was going nowhere in my *Speedo* cap.
Years ago, my classmates had swum
out of my depth. I clung to the side
and my one move of kicking up the broken
tail of my feet, my skin Brailleing.
Sometimes Mrs Harle threw me
her look, shouting once: 'What
would you have done at Zeebrugge?'

For fifty minutes every week I learned
the lesson of cold water. In summer
I sat out the gala, minding
the shed layers of other kids – even the babies
in armbands had thrown themselves in.
At nine I could fill a swimming pool
with the slow boats of excuse notes:

presiding over me were the twin lifeguards
of my mother and father. I can see them now
perched on the high board in clothes
eras older than them, a stovepipe and a stole.
They are clinging to each other, pretending to look
down on the girls who are not me – the sporty types
squealing and upsetting the applecart of the water.

27 Wood End

was older than home. It was where Dad felt
at home. Its cupboards were full of puzzles
with missing pieces. It was for ever, for six weeks
one summer, when Dad played
Mum, and Mum visited at weekends. The rest
of the time Dad's ancient aunties like Dorothy
were nearer. Tea was eggs and beans, and beans
and eggs and blackberries picked on canal walks
blighted by slugs and dark gaps between
stepping stones. The nearby market was hung
with rabbits, until Mum came on a Saturday
when it sold toys and records.

Above Wood End, Stoodley Pike
perched on a hill like an early god
surrounded by sheep and sheep-
shit. Its obelisk daggered the air above Dad
as he walked towards it, bowed by the enormity
of the rucksack like three kids on his shoulders.
Sometimes our heads were knocked together.
In the evenings we wrote diaries for Dad to look
back on when he was stuck at work, and we were quiet
during the news. Susan Maxwell was always on telly
– her lost face flickered in a far-off corner of Wood End –
a girl from up the road, about my age, but dead.

Darling Kisses

When we snogged, I was Mum's
trendy yoga friend Trish. You were Kev,
Trish's imagined fella. It was after *Dynasty*
when we kissed and 'did it'
by shaking our clothed bodies together
like Torvill and Dean in the *Bolero*.
'Darling Kisses' was our name for this –
you had to whisper 'Ooh Darling!' first.
We weren't close. We were on top of each other.

The massages began at Gran's house
with Mum-style tickling of the neck. Next came
animals traced down spines and my hand, just shy
of your forest – it was all teeth
and Disney wolves. I think of the forest
in Cardross with the ruined high-rise seminary
that in my childhood was a closed order. Today
its rooflessness is crowned by birds. Its altar
is an altar to needles and fallen angels and weather.

Fall

We wandered leisurely to the ruin
taking the cliff-side path in our stride,
our conversation strayed
from its usual setting. We split an apple,
sharing the taste of a moment's
windfall. In the background a helicopter
airlifted a climber – a woman – to safety.
This is my poem about being

pregnant. I like how ignorant
I am in it, caught out
up the coast from the rest of my life.
The father is in the office I christened
with him a couple of weeks earlier.
I am in a weekday's remote beauty spot,
carrying the child briefly
until I look down.

Dad and the Hen

How did I get here, sneaking
up on my father in nineteen-fifty?
I picture him looking like Christopher Robin
in bib shorts and buckle shoes.
He is kneeling over a much-loved hen –
pulling his hands away then
putting them back, pulling his hands away
then wringing its neck. Above his head, onions
grow spiders' legs – there are monsters
still hanging around the dark of Gran's shed.

Years later, Dad has always wanted
to keep hens. My parents' kitchen is feathered
with our childhood gifts of crayoned cockerels,
woolly birds that flop on the boiler with the battered tom.
'Hens make lovely pets. They give you eggs
then meat,' – Dad insists on the family joke.
'You could no more kill a pet than fly,' –
Mum bats back. Maybe she knows
nothing of the hen murder. Maybe even Dad has buried it.

I was seven, dipping into the perfect egg
when Gran opened a window in her bright pantry
and showed me Dad at my age – struggling
to kill his sick bird as she'd asked. She smiles fondly
and tells me of the poor job he made of it,
framed through the shed window. Now I am stuck keeking.
I see my little Dad kneeling up
in hen dust. Then I see him more clearly,
loving hens and hanging back on the edge of many things.

Gran's Chair

I could not take it when you died.
My sister kept your chair in the passage
of her flat while your discarded watch
conjured a carriage clock in that tired rent
of my late twenties, where I was living
(eating sleeping speaking into the damp mouth
of the house phone with its cable long-stretched
under the door) in one room as if it was lots
of rooms, going out looking for my own family
home at weekends in other people's bedrooms.

My thirties have been a landing; labouring
on the stairs to reach its strewn highway
in the early weeks of motherhood and now
my son charges naked down the runway
while I run after, trying to get him
ready. Your chair (which I carried awkwardly
into my house as if I was carrying you
but your chair) belongs in another era
and would be empty except for the unputaway
washing, decorating its worn nap like blossom.

Descendants

To my child I was born
at thirty-five. He does not know

a child is still curled up
inside of me, lost

in a book or leaning into
a brother and sister for a photo of a time

we were kids together under one roof.
My child does not know how recently

his father and I came to this solid
Victorian terrace or how comparatively

late and how we are following
our parents when we carry his body –

as a baby – up and down, up
and down the endless stairs.

Bedsocks; Willow
for G

After a 10k run and 9 years
of marriage you take my foot
in your hands and ease off one
of my bedsocks like a pair
of knickers here in our warm
living room where we always
are at the end of the day.
I have worn bedsocks
since bed became hard
a couple of years ago,
since sleep became
a fantastical figure
hidden under my side
of the bed or mewling
in the depths of the wardrobe,
since at night I failed
to take flight and started
hanging around the dark
kitchen or hanging off
your neck like a wingless
creature – since all that
got better I have hung on
to the bedsocks, the camomile tea
and the hot water bottle meaning
I may never again travel lightly.

Knowing this you ease off
my bedsock with its foolish
Primark hearts and hold my foot

in your hands and the naked
woman hidden in its sole
carefully stroking her jangling
nerve endings after nine years
of marriage and all that running.

Late Journey with my Father

I would put down my life like a book
I am halfway through and enjoy this journey
with my father as any old adults at a table
without the great landscape of my childhood
pressing at every window, and the carriages
rattling out their narrative we are stuck in.
I would have him not have to speak,
and me not have to listen to myself
calling his name *Daddy Dad* whatever
else I am saying. And this poem
would not have such a portentous title
with death signalled so overtly
as though Jenny Agutter is up the track
waving her scarlet bloomers but but
for the above (the landscape, the childhood,
the rattling) how would I know my father
on this crowded train which is not a Day Rover
ticket to eighties Blackpool, or him
seeing me halfway to university,
just an echo of those epic journeys –
us in place at the fixed table, sitting together
like this as our way of sitting together,
speaking together like this as is our way.

In Passing

Living where I grew up means I can be
sat at a window of the lofty new
library, thinking about my son starting
nursery, when my father strolls by
outside – wearing the big shoes he has
to now and holding a folder
of the marking he does in retirement.
I follow him from my seat on the shifting
centre of the city where his loaded body is
absorbed: *let me go*, it says, *the first*
of all the little fathers in your head.
I am not just hanging around your childhood's
street-corners. I need to be somewhere too.

Ten Ways to Remember Joe

At the library hatch, swigging tea for the worker
from a chipped Charles & Di mug – a decade after
they had split. Wheeling something to the other
side of campus. Humouring me and the rest
of the postgrads playing at being librarians
in the evenings on our way somewhere better.
Braced like TV strongmen from my childhood
but to lift books and bits of old university
furniture built by Vickers when the shipyards
were dying, rejected now by Health & Safety.
Waving hello/goodbye for ever on the corner
that time I was rushing to what I thought of
as my real life, which was just a lecture.
As the postbox on the corner – solid, everyday,
your true memorial. As the space beside
the postbox where you stood as though you are
hanging around in your absence showing me how
I too one day will disappear, and I am still rushing.
A portent. A Blue Riband eater. With a little toast
from Macbeth *I pray you, remember the porter.*

Work

These are the things I never wrote about –
the Nurofen. The smiley mug. *Postscript*
by Seamus Heaney blu-tacked to my bit
of wall. Nick hovering in the office
doorway as though he wasn't the boss.
Nick in his slippers sometimes.
The in tray where my twenties were to do.
The little window in the computer room
overlooking the houses I dreamed about
living in with my ex. The clock
where it was never home or lunch.
The clock whose hands I hung off
like the silent movie star in the poster
stuck in a hazy Freshers' Week bedroom.
In those days when nothing was connected
the slowest modem in. the. world.
The work skirt, Mum's cardie, the clogs
with gold studs I remember in detail
as if my history were no more substantial.
My getting the milk and phone *Hello
Gateway Communications*. The cheese
bites, strawberries dipped in chocolate,
lunches with lots of knives and glasses
on our birthdays when what we wanted
was a day off. The team meeting. The
low ceiling. Nick singing Here Comes
My Happiness Again (again and again).
These are the things I never wrote about
when I was starting to write or maybe
it was before my pen was my own

and writing was copy for Leech Homes
and press releases pending
the one tick two ticks of approval,
the stuff we went through after
Nick died, the mountain of stuff
he never got on top of and buried
under the weight of everything
that photo of him in his twenties
grinning and sticking up two fingers.

This poem would stop a stanza short
without Kate and I in a gallery café
a decade or so later on a weekday
which is not exactly a window
into my life but how it was that day.
This poem is a side, a plank of olives,
an unmade sandwich on a spread table –
we are discussing Emotional Labour,
ephemera, things that get left out
of archives. We are talking about YAY!
scribbled on a memo which for Kate
is YAY! conjures the boss uplifting
the whole team but for me is a wacky
hat, a happy dance, a clashing font,
too many exclamation marks, You Don't
Have to Be Mad etc or something
more like Morse, Like help, More like
help me please I'm drowning.

The Discovery Museum

Where stacks open on impermanent lanes
stuffed with birds though no birds sing:
the curator unfolds *Bewick's actual swan*;
hands out chaffinches; leads us like chicks
to an auk then a wildcat past the seals
and other creatures grazing our shins. Delving
into a box as if into my unconscious,
he deals me a bag of I-know-what; think
squirrel! to myself squirrel! before he can say
an extinct ship-rat from Sunderland. Dangling
the body like a shed evening glove by the tip
of one finger is how I become a woman
in this underground room who can handle a rat
(albeit a bagged rat; long since shuffled off).

The Gender and Law at Durham Research Group

are discussing provocation: holding law up to the light.
Their chairs clash at an inadequate table.
From the postgraduate student – her name written in silver
around her neck – to the professor who has brought cakes
out of her backpack – no one is afraid to use words
like contempt and coercion, or simply to shout
for milk or sugar if that is what they want.
This office is the opposite of a room with a low bed
where a woman might be held down so long.
I want to end with this office. I want to linger here all afternoon.

What Research Does

says you are not alone
even at your most alone

ill, bereaved, in a chair unable
to get out easily –

there are ninety-six of you
in this study alone –

teases out, makes connections,
speaks to the possibility of you
doing this or that, and the impossibility

opens a window in the stuffiness
of this office and summons you
with your sticks and grief,
with your every hesitation
recorded as qualitative evidence

Hex 1 says the researcher
(where Hex is Hexham and 1 is you
whose name has been redacted)
reports feeling confined, having given up
driving

Hex 2 stood in the garden
in the early days wondering
how everything could look the same
when the sky had fallen

brings you into the conversation
in this room which is not separate
from your own – this small meeting
space with its minutes and apologies
for absence and clock counting
down towards retirement and beyond
the door, the network of similar-looking
doors and corridors where everyone gets lost.

(T)here

Imagine someone who is no one
in particular in a chair or
on sticks unwilling or unable
to walk when they can no longer
drive. Imagine them having to
anyway; falling in the street
and someone helping them up,
saying what are you doing
out the house? – saying really
you shouldn't be out – Imagine
them going back in then
(with nowhere to go but in).

Imagine if you couldn't swim
being thrown in in
your seventies; or having been able
to swim all your life
being thrown by the swimmers coming towards you like fins
and by the kids who are just
throwing themselves in. Imagine
the panicky little flutter
of your feet in the water
and the eyes of the lifeguards
weighing you down. Imagine
being one of *those* people
who need the side and the side
slipping away until you are back
in the shallow end of your childhood
surrounded by posters shouting
NO RUNNING NO BOMBING NO
PETTING No Nothing. Imagine
swimming is walking, driving
or getting on a bus. It can
happen at any age, too.

That time in your twenties your hands stopped
working – curling back into a baby's fists-
you had to drop everything and *swore*
that if you ever got your old self back
you wouldn't take your hands for granted
but you would give   space
to the person travelling in front of you
tackling the enormity of the bus steps
and you did, for a while, and then you didn't.

(iv)

We need more rails more ramps more regular
services more seats and more people giving up
their seats more lanes more loos more or less
regulations and we need more people imagining
they are sitting next to their mother –
that it is their mother hanging on to the rail,
that their mother is the slowcoach holding up the bus:
even if they didn't get on with their mother,
she gave birth to you; it doesn't matter.

Back Yard

Still now your husband's absence is a room
you just walk into; any room in your house –
his not-thereness suspended like a starburst
light-fitting; his not-thereness a sudden
infestation – but the ceiling will not fall in
like a blanket covering the chairs of a den
for inside your walls are all the homes
your son will ever make. On a good night
you go out after bedtime into the yard
and sit with the baby monitor's static
under everything you do – notwithstanding
the strung-out washing-line, the creepy house
of the shed – this is the room that is open to you
where the world has been waiting on the sneck.
Beyond the cooling towers are fields. Now still.

Back Garden

All of my homes have been tents
pitched on this one's ancient grounds:
a patch of grass keeps the place
where my feet fell before they flew.
Among the leggy roses are the lost balls
and cats and fag-ends of a played-out
childhood. My father's sharp edges
and hammers are locked away, without
a key. He and my mother are in
their seventies, watching my son
begin to pull himself up on their furniture.

From the garden, I can see the room I had –
the solid desk by the window
where its airy reflection lodged in a tree.
Often my mother looked up
from her mowing, imagining
my room perhaps: now it is my son's
occasional nursery and still
full of my stuff. In a corner
of the garden, my husband wrestles
down ivy in our own back yard – trying
to shore up the little walls around our family.

Portrait of Dorothy Hodgkin as my
Mother with a Broken Hip

This study is everyday to you, says your homely cardie
and bowed unbrushed head; sat over your lofty work
in this portrait, as though over a poached egg. Pushed to one side
on your desk is a model of the molecular structure you untangled.
Although your room implies space, a window admits winter.
Tied by arthritis, your old hands reach for a pen; a book;
a magnifying glass – you have four hands to indicate
how busy you are and constrained. The extra limbs are the crutches
hooked over her chair (they are the grab rail, the bath board,
the perching stool et cetera). Your own hands are her leg sticking out
like an elephant in the room. Your gaze is hers, intent
on a Sudoku. To return to your desk, it is a flat universe which stops
at the unknown. Where she has never been, you summon her.
The bottom line in this poem is you look like my mother.

Facial

Softly painted by Fra Angelico,
as if by angels, are disembodied
hands on a wall of a monk's cell
in Florence that halo the holy face
– as it waits between blows –
with sticks and stones. That room
floats into my mind as the other

side of this one where I lie
like a little god, having stumbled
in after work. The air is full
of oils, and her hands
hover in the sacred space above
my prickled skin – touching me
just before they touch me again.

Dwelling

After fifteen years, I can remember
your cottage, steeped in the gathering
dark of the Northumberland countryside
on one of those early Friday evenings
in my twenties, with you
about to come in from work and me
getting unready: how naked
I look, composing my nakedness
in your bathroom's long mirror
and how my figure abides
in your house, which is just a lit
window now, set in my past.

Shrine

Cut away from your husband, children and sisters,
you are a tiny head in a flowery hat floating
in the huge doorstop of a glass photo frame
where I keep you because I have to keep you
somewhere these days after your death. I balance
your late likeness on the back bedroom sill so
that light comes in all around you – light
like the dark of a baby-scan with your face
the body at the off-centre of it all; your face
like Gala's face now caught in a Dalíesque
bardo of soft clocks and shed limbs. That hat
does nothing to pin you down or your eyes
off to one side as though you have seen
something outside of the everyday. 'All life ends
in little boxes,' says your son at the funeral
and that is true. Still, I light a scented candle and
will you to move up – up up up – out of this frame.

The walls are only there because you impute them

Most rooms are the bedroom the kitchen the living room,
full of the same old same old and afternoons, on top
of each other, never quite stacking up to be Home –
that is somewhere else or someone else or sometimes
just the light of other people's loving rooms as seen
on TV or from the street. Sometimes home seems little
more than a tent next to the estate of an old childhood.

We come to the Shrine Room late in the day
as though to learn to say *Bienvenue* say, or dance.
Your robes are the flashy orange of the last bus finally
pulling up in the driving rain. You ask us to sit
and contemplate our lack of inherent existence
then we have a cup of tea. Back home, the spare room
disappears when I close my eyes, remember what you said.

Illuminasia
Winter Gardens, Blackpool

little dragons stream towards me snap
snapping their jaws as if, still my hands

would shield my face. I know dragons
don't exist but fear like love is

like this – projection in a darkened room –
and I am always seeing dragons where

there are pussy cats or where there is
nothing at all as though I am always

seeing through silly specs even outside
of this exhibition with its illuminations

Liminal
Manjushri KMC, Ulverston

She lives near the temple, her nest-egg helped build;
now her wealth is a bit of gold leaf she can see
from the window of her little. Every evening

when the world is at prayer or peeling potatoes,
she creeps out; a monk's robe is to her fleece
as his tonsure is to her topknot of rats-tails.

She has many mouths to feed and a
bottomless bucket: in her heart she is
serving all sentient beings – the murine gods

that scamper in the far-flung Indian temple
as much as the common or garden Cumbrian
rodents, which are huge in these parts.

The Durrell Wildlife Park

Jersey. Because I was not ready
to go abroad but almost
after a year of one day
at a time. We left the hotel
with its tired rooms
where everyone has not slept
to visit the zoo's transparent cages.
(the bears lay apart within)
I felt the nearness of their breathing,
their eyes speaking to me
like the strange jungle plant
of *cloudforest snowline warm savanna*
worlds beyond the walled existence
all of us bang our heads against
sooner or later and from nowhere.

Ulverston Sands

Bagged in clear plastic and held
down by a handful of pebbles
arranged in a heart-shape,
your photo is a sign
you were last anywhere here.
Fiona remembers the tale of you
(which is last year's tale)
a young man from the nearby
Buddhist Festival disappeared
through the quicksand
into afternoon's meditative silence.
How I like to write about Fiona
in this poem in her waterproof
snapping a chunky *KitKat*
as she tells me monks still
prostrate here in your wake.
For want of any great conclusion
I would end with a line of monks
in their orange robes like so
many Squirrel Nutkins bobbing
against a vast watery horizon.

Colony
Tyrone Guthrie Centre, Ireland

Life was a big fat waterlily that day on the boat
with Lisa and Emer with a life-jacket sprung up
around me as orange and bright as the gown
of a monk who has realised happiness (work
was in another country – filed like the course work
my brother used to stow under a bush overnight
before heading to the pub; it never went anywhere).

Ducked out for fresh air from the Big House
where we had a month for writing and writing
was under every tureen and writing was calling
beneath the eaves and writing was the niggly pea
and all of the cushy mattresses, or music was or art;
everyone was an artist in that impermanent house
and blown in to stay for a little while like Poppins.

After a thousand aeons maybe, a blind turtle
will surface in a choppy ocean to stick its head
through the golden yoke of a precious human life:
and here I am on the photo, just bobbing around
in my life-jacket. Years after, even after settling
down, I thought of happiness as that day on the lake –
not writing, but gambolling, inside art's great estate.

Beginners Meditation

The door to the Compassion Centre is locked.
We keep trying its handle; pressing our faces
against the big window where the Buddha is
unmoved among flowers. Thwarted on the Path
to Enlightenment, we linger opposite *Domino's*
and *Lily Ladies Leisure* – wanting a monk to emerge
from the rush-hour like a brightly coloured bus
with our number. Soon we will give up
on our class and go back to our everyday lives
but, for now, on this lovely evening lifted
from a childhood, it is not yet late; somewhere
a shadow of ourselves might still be playing out.

Acknowledgements

Many thanks to the editors of the following magazines and anthologies where some of these poems first appeared:

The North, Oxford Poetry, Poetry Ireland Review, The Poetry Review, Poetry Wales, Reader, The Rialto, Stand, Hallelujah for 50ft Women (Raving Beauties/Bloodaxe, 2015), *The Poetics of the Archive* (Newcastle Centre for the Literary Arts, 2015).

Thank you to The Society of Authors Authors' Foundation for an award in 2017.

The sequence *(T)here* first appeared on 100 First York buses in 2017. I am grateful to the Co-Motion Centre at the University of York and University of Newcastle for a residency that made this possible. *(T)here* was also exhibited at York Explore and Newcastle City Libraries.

An abridged version of *Work* came second in the 2017 Ledbury Poetry Competition.

I wrote *Poem for the Archive* for Newcastle University's Bloodaxe Archive Project in 2015.

Beginners' Meditation came second in the 2014 McLellan Poetry Competition.

I wrote *The Gender and Law at Durham Research Group* and
27, *Wood End* during a residency at Durham University Law
School in 2012 funded by The Leverhulme Trust.

Thank you to New Writing North for a *Time to Write* Award
in 2011.

NEW FICTION FROM SALT

RON BUTLIN
Billionaires' Banquet (978-1-78463-100-0)

NEIL CAMPBELL
Sky Hooks (978-1-78463-037-9)

SUE GEE
Trio (978-1-78463-061-4)

CHRISTINA JAMES
Rooted in Dishonour (978-1-78463-089-8)

V.H. LESLIE
Bodies of Water (978-1-78463-071-3)

WYL MENMUIR
The Many (978-1-78463-048-5)

ALISON MOORE
Death and the Seaside (978-1-78463-069-0)

ANNA STOTHARD
The Museum of Cathy (978-1-78463-082-9)

STEPHANIE VICTOIRE
The Other World, It Whispers (978-1-78463-085-0)

RECENT FICTION FROM SALT

KERRY HADLEY-PRYCE
The Black Country (978-1-78463-034-8)

CHRISTINA JAMES
The Crossing (978-1-78463-041-6)

IAN PARKINSON
The Beginning of the End (978-1-78463-026-3)

CHRISTOPHER PRENDERGAST
Septembers (978-1-907773-78-5)

MATTHEW PRITCHARD
Broken Arrow (978-1-78463-040-9)

JONATHAN TAYLOR
Melissa (978-1-78463-035-5)

GUY WARE
The Fat of Fed Beasts (978-1-78463-024-9)

This book has been typeset by
SALT PUBLISHING LIMITED
using Sabon, a font designed by Jan Tschichold
for the D. Stempel AG, Linotype and Monotype
Foundries. It is manufactured using Creamy 70gsm, a
Forest Stewardship Council™ certified paper from Stora
Enso's Anjala Mill in Finland. It was printed and bound
by Clays Limited in Bungay, Suffolk, Great Britain.

CROMER
GREAT BRITAIN
MMXVIII